BEATING BURNOUT

Based on *The Burnout Bible* by Rachel Philpotts

First published in Great Britain by Practical Inspiration Publishing, 2026

ISBN 978-1-78860-892-3 (paperback)
978-1-78860-893-0 (ebook)

EU GPSR representative: LOGOS EUROPE, 9 rue Nicolas Poussin, LA ROCHELLE 17000, France Contact@logoseurope.eu.

Contents

Series introduction

Welcome to *6-Minute Smarts*!

This is a series of very short books with one simple purpose: to introduce you to ideas that can make life and work better, and to give you time and space to think about how those ideas might apply to *your* life and work.

Each book introduces you to ten powerful ideas, but ideas on their own are useless – that's why each idea is followed by self-coaching questions to help you work out the 'so what?' for you in just six minutes of exploratory writing. What's exploratory writing? It's the kind of writing you do just for yourself, fast and free, without worrying what anyone else thinks. It's not just about getting ideas out of your head and onto paper where you can see them; it's about finding new connections and insights as you write. This is where the magic happens.

Whatever you're facing, there's a *6-Minute Smarts* book just for you. And once you've learned how to coach yourself through a new idea, you'll be smarter for life.

Find out more...

Introduction

Picture a fierce female. To all intents and purposes, she is at the top of her game, killing it at work and spinning all the plates at home. Now really look at her. Her eyes are vacant, her smile is forced and her clothes are tight. She is constantly run down and tired all the damn time. She has lost her glow. Behind closed doors she is tearful and withdrawing from social activities. She is frustrated and can't seem to tap into the same motivation and energy reserves she had previously. She knows something is wrong but she keeps going, just doing what she can to survive. She can't see it, but she's on the brink of burnout.

How many of us, if we're honest, recognize ourselves in this picture, whether now or in the past? If not us then we all know someone else who has felt this way. Taking it one step further, how many of us are brave enough to admit it out loud?

If it helps, I'll go first. I was that girl: fierce on the outside, broken on the inside. I burnt out.

In my 30s my work hard, play hard lifestyle began to take its toll. The workload and pressure became relentless at a time when I was already feeling the isolation of senior management and the frustration of the ever-present glass ceiling. My mood plummeted and I was plagued by negative self-talk – telling myself that I wasn't good enough, that I was a failure. I found myself missing personal appointments and disengaging from my family and friends. I instinctively knew something was wrong but didn't want to admit it to myself out of fear. I just tried to keep going, keep working, keep achieving – until one day I couldn't anymore. I broke.

It wasn't dramatic. It all happened behind closed doors. I just woke up one day unable to function. I didn't go to work, instead hiding myself away for several months. Even then I didn't know what had happened. The doctors said I was depressed, and I believed them. I felt depressed. Well, actually, I felt nothing. I was too damn exhausted. I had burnt out.

I was medically signed-off for six months and it was during my time of convalescence that I discovered the concept of functional medicine. I learned how stress messes with all biological function, especially brain function. I learned how essential nutrition is for health. Perhaps most importantly, I learned about myself. Specifically, how the combination of my individual biochemistry, genetic predisposition and life thus far could determine my personal diet and lifestyle needs and also explain how I had arrived at burnout. I was fascinated.

I began eating a whole-food diet and practising self-care through exercise, yoga and relaxation. After a few months, the dark clouds lifted and my weight also began to normalize. I was no longer bloated and I had more energy than I'd had in years. I was starting to feel like me again.

I decided to leave the corporate world and go back to university for retraining. I had a special interest in how to treat – and, more importantly, prevent – stress-related mood disorders such as burnout, so I immersed myself in health and nutrition science, biochemistry and neurobiology. Three years of clinical training and a master's degree later I was ready to fulfil my life's purpose: to help other 'tired and wired' career women to combat the fatigue and emotional overwhelm of burnout naturally.

I now run my own functional medicine clinic doing just that, creating ultra-personalized health programmes for patients incorporating therapeutic supplements, diet and lifestyle change and stress-management techniques.

The results never cease to amaze me and that's why I decided to write this book. Although a book can never replicate the clinic experience, I hope that in sharing my knowledge of burnout, its root causes and how it can be managed naturally, I can arm you with the knowledge to either prevent burnout or stop it in its tracks by making manageable changes to your diet and lifestyle.

Before we begin, I need to let you know that the information and guidance provided in this book is for information purposes only. This book is not a substitute for any consultation, diagnosis or medical treatment given by your doctor or other healthcare provider. You must not rely on any information or guidance provided in this book as an alternative to medical advice from your doctor or healthcare provider.

If you think you may be suffering from any medical condition, you should seek immediate medical attention from your healthcare provider. Do not delay seeking medical advice, disregard medical advice or discontinue medical treatment because of information or guidance provided in this book.

Now that all the formalities are done, let's begin.

Day 1
What is burnout?

When I asked a group of high-achieving career women to tell me what they thought of when they heard the word 'burnout', they described exhaustion, anxiety and overwhelm. When we dug a little deeper, feelings of fear, frustration and failure emerged. Some described feeling depressed, lacking in motivation and losing interest in their career. I heard stories of horrible bosses, being overlooked for promotion and confrontational colleagues, accompanied by strained relationships at home and social withdrawal. When I asked what other symptoms they had noticed at the time, many reported problems sleeping, irritable bowel syndrome (IBS), menstrual disturbances, infertility and frequent infections. But they had not connected these symptoms to stress and were surprised to learn that these are all symptoms of burnout.

In the UK, burnout is not medically recognized. If you search for 'burnout' on the NHS website, it returns no results. But there is widespread recognition of burnout as an occupational syndrome. The World Health Organization classifies burnout as an 'occupational phenomenon' in the 11th revision of its International Classification of Diseases (ICD-11), though it doesn't recognize it as a distinct medical condition: 'Burnout is a syndrome conceptualized as resulting from chronic workplace stress that has not been successfully managed.'[1]

These were some of the symptoms I personally experienced before and at the point of burnout:

- Exhaustion
- Overwhelm
- Nervous tension
- Mood swings
- Insomnia
- Anxiety
- Depression
- Difficulty concentrating
- Brain fog
- Loss of motivation and drive
- Weight gain

- Bloating/IBS
- Sugar cravings
- PCOS
- Irregular menstrual cycles
- Anaemia
- Frequent infections
- Low blood pressure
- Blurred vision and dizziness
- Blackouts and fainting fits.

The three stages of burnout

Burnout doesn't just happen overnight. HPA-axis (hypothalamic–pituitary–adrenal axis) dysregulation and adrenal insufficiency build up over time with a collection of physiological effects that can be grouped together in three stages, which can be thought of as a Venn diagram:

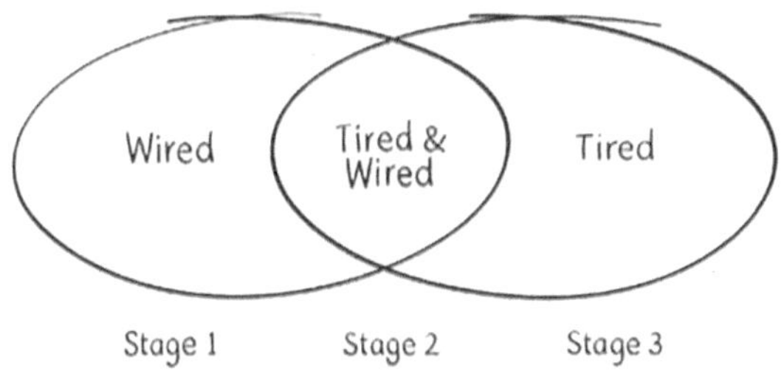

Stage 1: Wired

This is the coping stage, the sensation of being on high alert, perhaps a little anxious. The first stage of burnout is noticing that you are feeling this way constantly. The health consequences of this stage may appear mild compared to the later stages, but I'd argue that Stage 1 is actually the most critical phase of burnout.

Stage 2: Tired *and* wired

At some stage, the body loses resilience and is less able to cope, disturbing the delicate balance of the HPA axis. The brain doesn't know when or if to press the stop button on the stress response. The adrenal glands are still receiving signals from the brain via the pituitary gland and continue to pump out cortisol, but cortisol receptors are becoming less sensitive, meaning more cortisol must be produced to achieve the same energy levels and focus. As a result, agitation, being on edge and tiredness increase.

Stage 3: Tired

This is more like total exhaustion and emotional overwhelm. The demand on the stress response has outstripped supply and sub-optimal adrenal function has occurred. Signalling from the brain is dysregulated and cortisol production has declined. Mentally and physically exhausted, this is a low cortisol or hypocortisolaemic state.

(NB I've called them stages 1–3 but this doesn't mean they occur in this precise order in a path to burnout. We use cortisol level testing to determine what stage our clients are at.)

While the biochemical causes and effects of burnout are complex and unique to each individual, there is one common driver: chronic stress. So that's where we'll start tomorrow.

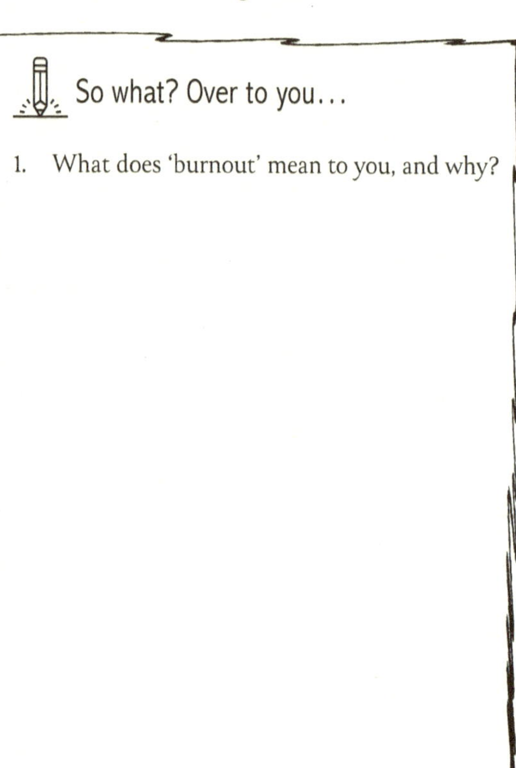

So what? Over to you…

1. What does 'burnout' mean to you, and why?

2. Which, if any, of the symptoms listed above do you notice in yourself?

3. Do you see yourself in one of the three stages of burnout described here? How?

Day 2

Stress – the invisible trigger

Most of us think of stress as part of everyday life. We joke about being stressed, wear it like a badge of honour or tell ourselves it's just the way things are. But too often it's quietly wreaking havoc on our bodies and minds.

What is stress?

We typically use the word 'stress' to refer both to things that have got us worked up (an incessant workload, a presentation to the board) and to the feelings we associate with that pressure (anxiety, tension, fatigue, overwhelm, etc). The former we might refer to as stressors and the latter as a stressed-out psychological state. Good stress is the excitement and challenge that comes with a new project or the motivational effect of a deadline; bad stress is usually associated with overload or a negative situation (distress).

Stress can extend beyond the workplace: watching the news, scrolling on social media, poor health, illness or injury, nutrient deficiencies, stimulants, loneliness, exercise and junk food are all environmental stressors that many of us are exposed to daily. Your brain doesn't care what the stressor is, it puts them all in the 'threat' category and responds accordingly.

In the body, stress is a physiological state that occurs in response to an external or internal challenge or threat. It's our body's way of making adjustments to ensure survival. It's an adaptive process; we develop resilience so that we're better able to anticipate and cope with the same challenge next time around. Problems only occur when the body's systems are chronically challenged or stressed. This can lead to inappropriate adjustments and a maladaptive state, which can contribute to chronic disease.

Stress and your brain

Your brain is the key organ that orchestrates your stress response. The brain determines what's stressful, regulates your physiological and behavioural responses to cope with the stressor and rewires itself to function differently next time – learning from the experience. This rewiring can either be helpful (adaptive) or unhelpful (maladaptive).

In executing the stress response the brain is supported by various biological systems, primarily:

- The HPA axis
- The autonomic nervous system
- The metabolic system
- The immune system
- The gut.

Each of these systems produces biochemical mediators of the stress response (hormones, neurotransmitters, cytokines, etc), which collectively regulate one another.

Let's say your brain recognizes a threat. It will initiate what's known as the 'fight or flight' response. First, lightning-fast signals are sent via the autonomic nervous system to the adrenal medulla instructing it to release noradrenaline and adrenaline. These neurotransmitters act to raise the internal threat level to high. Second, the adaptive coping mechanism is launched by the neuroendocrine system, known as the HPA axis. Specifically, the adrenal cortex releases our stress hormone cortisol in response to signals from the hypothalamus and pituitary glands in the brain.

The result of HPA axis activation is a cascade of physiological effects that prepare the body to deal with perceived threat or danger: mobilization of energy, relaxation of the airways, dilation of pupils, increase in heart rate. At the same time, the fight or flight response inhibits non-essential biological processes such as digestion, reproduction and repair. Our natural stress response down-regulates digestion, reproduction and repair.

What our brains consider to be stressful is all a matter of perception and is regulated by its different areas. The prefrontal cortex is responsible for receiving information from the environment and internally interpreting and categorizing this data. If it decides a disgruntled customer is worth stressing about, it will alert the hypothalamus to initiate the stress response.

Stress and your adrenal glands

Your adrenal glands, located above each kidney, are perhaps most widely known for regulating your response to stress; however, they also secrete hormones that are responsible for regulating your circadian rhythm, blood pressure and electrolyte balance, blood sugar balance and metabolism, suppressing the immune system and controlling inflammation.

Chronic stress places considerable strain on the adrenal glands and ultimately affects the body's ability to adapt and cope. This can lead to HPA axis dysregulation and adrenal insufficiency – in other words, burnout.

Chronic stress

Historically, the fight or flight response enabled humans to flee from predators or fight off a bear. Once the brain recognizes that the threat has passed it hits the stop button on the stress response. Cortisol levels return to normal and digestive, reproductive and immune function resume.

These days, stress is a daily, even hourly, occurrence. It's rarely as life-threatening as a bear attack, but now we might experience:

- Frequent stressors throughout the day, necessitating the brain to frequently activate/deactivate the stress response
- Prolonged stressors with no apparent ending, so the brain doesn't know when or if it is over and never presses stop
- Overwhelm and a total inability to cope with the load.

All of these scenarios can lead to unhelpful rewiring of the brain and leave us lacking the protective effects of a normal adaptive stress response.

Scientists call the accumulated 'wear and tear' of chronic stress allostatic load. Allostasis is the process of achieving stability through change, but chronic allostatic load means your body's systems are paying a heavy price for staying on high alert.

Signs of allostatic overload include:

- Persistent fatigue
- Poor sleep, trouble waking or staying asleep
- Difficulty concentrating ('brain fog')
- Heightened anxiety or irritability
- Digestive issues
- Frequent infections or slow recovery from illness.

The longer you stay in a state of chronic stress, the more these symptoms become your 'new normal'.

Naming and recognizing the hidden effects of stress is the first step in taking back control. Tomorrow, we'll look more closely at why women are especially vulnerable to burnout and how gendered patterns and expectations make stress even harder to escape.

So what? Over to you…

1. What's your relationship with stress?

2. In what ways do you experience both good and bad stress?

3. Which, if any, signs of allostatic overload do you recognize?

Day 3

Why women burn out more

Burnout is not a uniquely female experience; however, women are more likely than men to experience emotional exhaustion in business and are at increased risk of burnout.[2] Why? Well, we don't fully understand yet, partly because most of the historical research on stress has been conducted by men on male subjects.

Psychologist Shelley Taylor has proposed that rather than 'fight or flight', women may have a 'tend and befriend' stress response, tapping into biological care-giving and attachment systems that push us to focus not only on our own survival but also that of our offspring.[3]

That tendency might increase women's vulnerability to burnout. For example, climbing the career ladder can be an isolating experience that reduces women's capacity for socializing outside of work. It may also result in either delaying starting a family or having less time to spend with them. (On the flip side, this theory may also suggest ways to reduce the risk of burnout – being able to lean on your 'girl gang' in times of need is both a protective mechanism and a way of managing stress.)

Environmental factors

Burnout risk doesn't just come down to gender or individual vulnerability. Environmental factors both at work and at home can influence susceptibility to burnout. At work, burnout-related factors can be classified as either increasing the risk of burnout (work demands) or mitigating the risk of burnout (work resources). Typical demands that we all recognize as stressful include long hours or irregular shift patterns, job uncertainty, abusive supervision and interpersonal conflict.

Even in an age of so-called gender equality, it's easy to see how the balance might be tipped unfavourably against women. Despite ongoing efforts to equalize pay, the gender pay gap still exists and, interestingly, becomes wider as we enter our 30s and 40s. And just as that gap begins to widen, we face major life decisions about careers and babies. Having chosen a path, we risk dissatisfaction in the life area we leave behind – or we try to do it all, each path increasing the risk of burnout in susceptible women. As Joy Burnford points out in her book, *Don't Fix Women*, there are many obstacles on the path![4]

Women are still more likely to be the primary caregiver for children and therefore more likely to experience work–home conflict. Women are also more likely to take on work they are overqualified for in an attempt to strike a better work–life balance and are more likely to be overlooked for promotion, which reduces their sense of control and purpose.

Part-time and flexible working is the modern way of attempting to address the issue of work–life balance and, indeed, these arrangements can offer protective effects in the short term. (Beauregard et al. found that female burnout levels were reduced when participants had more time outside of work to invest in domestic tasks.[5]) However, part-time work also presents with career limitations that may not be helpful to female occupational mental health and a sense of fulfilment in the long term.

And then we arrive at mid-life, staring down the menopause while getting paid less than our male counterparts. It's not hard to see why women are more stressed and more likely to experience occupational exhaustion, cynicism and reduced efficacy – the core characteristics of burnout.

Hormonal factors

We'll look at hormones in more detail in Day 6, but it's worth noting here that women's lives are marked by a series of significant hormonal changes – puberty, pregnancy, postpartum, perimenopause and menopause – all of which can have profound effects on mood, energy and stress resilience. These life stages can increase vulnerability to burnout, especially when combined with external stressors.

The hormonal fluctuations associated with the menstrual cycle, pregnancy and menopause can all affect brain chemistry and stress tolerance. For example, declining oestrogen levels during perimenopause and menopause can impact the regulation of mood and increase susceptibility to anxiety and depression.

It's the intersection of these biological, psychological and social factors that makes women more vulnerable to burnout. But burnout is by no means *only* a problem for women.

Tomorrow, we'll look at how burnout affects brain and body function – and what that means for recovery.

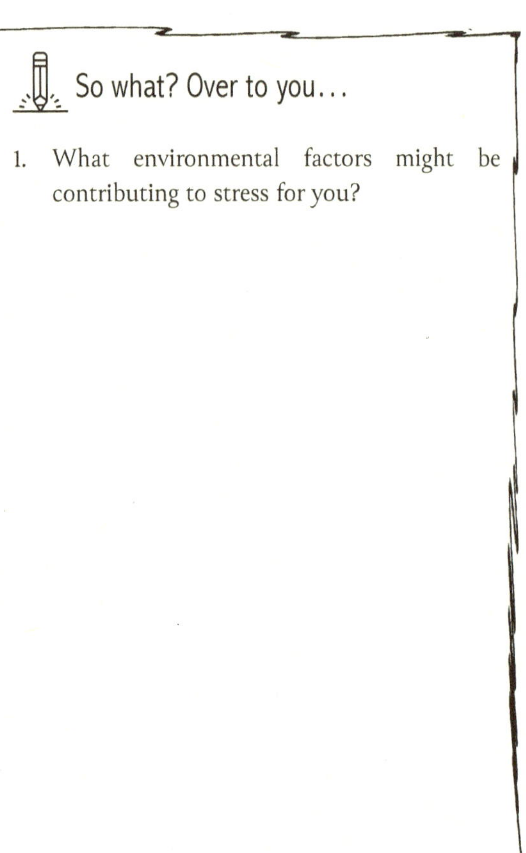

So what? Over to you...

1. What environmental factors might be contributing to stress for you?

2. Where are the opportunities for you to build 'befriend' support into your life?

3. What stage of life are you at, and how might that be impacting?

Day 4
From brain fog to breakdown

Burnout often begins with vague symptoms that can be hard to interpret. If you took them to a doctor, it's likely you'd be misdiagnosed with general anxiety or major depressive disorder. But it's important that you learn to recognize these early warning signs as signals from the body and brain because the outcomes as burnout takes hold can be very serious.

The cost of burnout

Poor cognitive function

One of the earliest and most overlooked symptoms of burnout is poor cognitive function – what many people call 'brain fog'. Your prefrontal cortex (PFC), the area of your brain that controls the highest levels of cognitive function and your thoughts, behaviours and emotions, is affected by both fatigue and anxiety. PFC dysfunction can show up as:

- Difficulty concentrating
- Poor decision making
- Poor recall/forgetfulness
- Reduced insight and judgement
- Reduced empathy and compassion
- Reduced optimism and persistence
- Reduced self-regulation and inhibitory control.

Sound familiar? All of these impair professional performance and increase occupational cynicism, both of which define burnout. Perhaps more concerningly, chronic stress can actually destroy grey matter, reducing PFC volume while simultaneously activating more primitive brain circuitry in the amygdala – your 'fear centre'.

Mood disorders

Over-production of the stress hormone cortisol (as seen in Stage 1 and 2 burnout) have been linked with 'melancholic depression', which is characterized by feeling anxious throughout the day, insomnia, feelings of dread and lack of appetite. Under-production of cortisol, meanwhile, is associated with 'atypical depression', characterized by overwhelming fatigue, lethargy, excessive sleep and increased appetite/overeating.[6]

As well as atypical depression, suppressed cortisol patterns have been linked with other mood disorders such as seasonal affective disorder, panic disorder, bipolar II, postpartum depression and generalized anxiety disorder.[7]

Fatigue

Another hallmark of burnout as it progresses is overwhelming fatigue. The exhaustion of Stage 3 burnout shares many characteristics with chronic fatigue syndrome, or myalgic encephalomyelitis (ME), a long-term, debilitating condition that leaves sufferers unable to engage effectively in day-to-day tasks. Common symptoms include extreme fatigue, sleep issues, cognitive issues, muscle aches, palpitations and headaches. The exact causes are unknown, but psychological stress, hormone imbalance and immune dysregulation are thought to play a role.

Autoimmune conditions

Perhaps one of the biggest impacts of chronic stress is on our immune system. Physiological stress is pro-inflammatory and decreases our ability to launch an anti-inflammatory counter response. Low levels of chronic stress that persist for years leave us susceptible to frequent infections and colds and vulnerable to developing chronic disease.[8]

IBS and 'leaky gut'

The brain and the gut can communicate both ways in what is known as the gut–brain axis (more about this in Day 7). Consequently, stress can influence gut functioning and has been linked with IBS and irritable bowel diseases (IBD) such as Crohn's and ulcerative colitis.[9] Stress may also be a factor in changing the composition of the gut microbiome, and may lead to the gut becoming 'leaky' or more permeable.[10] 'Leaky gut' has been linked with systemic conditions such as arthritis, migraine and acne.[11]

Cardiovascular disease

The stress response raises our blood pressure and dilates blood vessels so that oxygen from the lungs can rapidly reach our muscles to enable fight or flight. Chronic activation of the stress response over time has been linked with hypertension (high blood pressure) and diminished endothelial function, where the arteries narrow instead of remaining open. Both hypertension and cardiovascular disease increase the risk of heart attack and stroke. In these cases, stress can be fatal.[12]

Obesity and the metabolic syndrome

Chronic stress increases the risk of obesity and a collection of conditions known as metabolic syndrome – the precursors of type 2 diabetes and cardiovascular disease.

Cortisol stimulates our appetite and increases our preference for sugary, high-fat foods. Consumed in excess, these types of foods may contribute to blood sugar dysregulation and increased fat storage, particularly around the abdomen.[13] Excess cortisol is converted into cortisone, which is stored in fat cells – particularly in the abdominal area. In a vicious circle, excess abdominal fat equals more space to store cortisol, and increased cortisol increases fat. This is why we often develop a 'burnout belly'. It can take years to get rid of this. (Believe me, I'm still working on mine!)

Infertility and pregnancy

In survival mode, reproduction is considered non-essential and hormone production is down-regulated. Our libido is decreased and our menstrual cycle might go on the fritz or disappear altogether, so obviously chronic stress may impair fertility outcomes.

Elevated cortisol has also been associated with early pregnancy loss, miscarriage, foetal distress and pre-term birth.[14] Maternal stress can impact the temperament and cognitive function of babies after birth and may even reduce their resilience to stress and increase their susceptibility to disease in adulthood.[15]

That's why it's so important to tackle burnout and get stress under control if you're thinking about pregnancy.

Cancer

Finally, the dreaded big one. Emerging research suggests that chronic daily stress, severe life events and social isolation, which are all stressors on the human body, may play a role in the growth and spread of cancer. The human stress response suppresses immune function, creating the right environment for cancer cell growth, while simultaneously preventing the natural process of cell die-off. In one study, female rodents, exposed to the psychosocial stress of isolation, experienced increased growth and malignancy of breast cancer, compared to rodents who lived in a group.[16] As well as being more tumour-prone, the stressed rodents exhibited hyper-vigilant behaviours like anxiety and fearfulness. In humans, dysregulated or flattened cortisol patterns (like those observed in Stage 3 burnout) have been associated with increased mortality rates from metastatic breast cancer.[17]

The good news

The symptoms we experience are actually our body's warning signs, prompting us to change our behaviour in order to restore balance. When these symptoms are just ignored, burnout is able to flourish. But the good news is that research shows recovery is possible.

In Day 5, we'll dig deeper into how burnout changes our mood chemistry, and what practical steps we can take to restore balance.

So what? Over to you…

1. Which of these symptoms resonates most with you?

2. What would it mean to you to address these symptoms?

3. How might you prepare yourself to take action?

Day 5
Your mood chemistry

Burnout is more than exhaustion. It's a biochemical state – a shift in the brain's delicate chemistry. The key players are three powerful brain chemicals: serotonin, dopamine and melatonin. Their balance determines how we feel, think, sleep and cope.

The mood molecules: serotonin, dopamine and melatonin

Serotonin is often called the 'happy hormone'. It stabilizes mood, supports healthy sleep, helps regulate appetite and underpins emotional resilience. Dopamine is our anticipation and reward neurotransmitter; it's closely linked to how much pleasure we feel and our motivation levels. Melatonin is our sleep hormone, critical for rest and repair.

Serotonin is produced mainly in the gut (about 90%) and to a lesser extent in the brain. Dopamine is produced in several regions of the brain, but the prefrontal cortex and the reward pathway are especially important for energy, motivation and cognitive performance. Melatonin is produced in the pineal gland, mostly at night, and regulates our circadian rhythm.

Each interacts with the others. When the system's in harmony, we feel well. When stress or poor nutrition disrupts the balance, the effects ripple out across mind and body.

How stress and nutrition disrupt mood chemistry

Under chronic stress, the brain's ability to make and use these chemicals is compromised. Over time, this results in low mood, poor motivation, cravings, brain fog and disturbed sleep.

Stress also increases inflammation in the brain and body, reducing the availability of tryptophan (the amino acid building block for serotonin and melatonin). If your diet is low in high-quality protein, or your digestion is impaired by stress, you won't have enough raw materials to make the chemicals that make you feel good.

The serotonin story

Serotonin is made from tryptophan, an essential amino acid that cannot be produced in the body and therefore must be obtained from the food we eat. Unfortunately, tryptophan is one of the least abundant amino acids in our food supply and it competes with other amino acids for absorption and transfer across the blood–brain barrier, making us vulnerable to deficiency.

This is why it's super important to eat protein – and particularly protein sources that are higher in tryptophan such as eggs, salmon, turkey and other poultry, chickpeas, nuts and organic soy.

Assuming there's sufficient tryptophan available to make serotonin, certain 'helper' vitamins and minerals are also needed as 'co-factors' to undertake the conversion process from tryptophan to serotonin: adequate iron, magnesium, zinc and vitamin B6. As you can see, optimum nutrition is needed for optimal mood. Some serotonin is made in the gut to regulate motility and inflammation. The rest is made in the brain, where it stabilizes mood, reduces anxiety and helps us manage stress.

Dopamine: the drive and focus neurotransmitter

Dopamine is our anticipation and reward neurotransmitter; it's closely linked to how much pleasure we feel and our motivation levels. Imbalances in dopamine may present as some of the symptoms we're already familiar with: difficulty concentrating, low motivation levels, agitation and reward-seeking/ addictive behaviours (do you reach for the chocolate or wine when you're feeling stressed?). Both low and high dopamine levels – influenced by genetics, diet and/or lifestyle – have been linked with anxiety, lethargy, mood swings and depression in the scientific literature.[18]

Like other neurotransmitters, dopamine is derived from an amino acid – in this case tyrosine – and requires key nutrients as co-factors in its synthesis: folate and vitamins D and B6. Low dopamine levels may result from nutrient deficiency.

Dopamine and serotonin are closely linked and imbalances in one of these neurotransmitters may affect the levels of the other.

Melatonin: the sleep hormone

Melatonin is also reliant on tryptophan for synthesis. There is a reciprocal relationship among sleep, energy levels and mood. Have you ever felt so wired or emotionally overwhelmed that you just couldn't fall asleep, only to then feel tired, grumpy and tearful the next morning because you haven't slept? You just manage to get going by mid-afternoon only to find yourself in the same spiral later on. It's an exhausting cycle that can take its toll on our mental health and can ultimately contribute to burnout.

Melatonin works in tandem with cortisol and has an opposing rhythm. Whereas cortisol peaks in the morning to give us our 'get up and go' and then steadily declines throughout the day, melatonin is designed to be at lower levels in the morning and higher in the evening to prepare us for sleep. An imbalance in one or both of these signalling hormones can contribute to insomnia or disrupted sleep patterns.

These three mood hormones aren't the only factors in your brain chemistry: there's a whole raft of neurotransmitters, hormones and chemicals such as neurotrophins and neuropeptides in the mix. But one factor that's common to them all is that how you eat massively affects their balance and therefore your mood. See Day 9 for more advice on how to eat to boost your mood!

Supporting your mood chemistry means seeing symptoms as signals, a reminder to nourish your brain.

In Day 6, we'll look at hormones – the other major driver of burnout symptoms – and how to bring them back into balance.

So what? Over to you…

1. Which mood symptoms (low motivation, poor sleep, cravings, brain fog) are most familiar to you right now?

2. What is one small nutrition or lifestyle change you could make this week to support your brain chemistry?

3. How might you begin tracking your symptoms as feedback?

Day 6
Hormone havoc

Your hormones can play havoc with your mood. And working and playing hard can take its toll on how well your hormones function. Basically, balanced hormones are the key to successful communication in the body. Mixed-up chemical messaging leads to mental (and physical) chaos and confusion.

Hormones also have a starring role in burnout prevention and the stress response. If the brain is the director, then cortisol – your survival hormone – is the leading lady.

When cortisol is active, the production of many other hormones is affected. This is a natural part of adaption to keep you safe. But when cortisol levels are chronically high, like we see in Stage 2 burnout, or woefully low as in Stage 3 burnout, wider hormone dysregulation is possible. This is why the symptoms of burnout can extend way beyond feeling 'tired and wired'.

Obviously, hormones and endocrinology are such vast topics that we can't cover them in detail here. But the hormones that have the biggest impact on mood balance and those that are affected the most by burnout are:

- Cortisol – because of its role in our stress responses
- Insulin – because of its interplay with cortisol in regulating blood sugar levels
- Thyroid hormones – because of their influence on the chemicals in our autonomic nervous system (dopamine, noradrenaline, adrenaline)
- Reproductive hormones – because of their influence on our mood and energy levels.

Women are often predisposed to think negatively about hormones, mainly because we face menstruation each month. I believe that the more informed we are about hormone health, the more we can reframe our thinking about hormones and begin to embrace them as the life-giving, burnout-protective chemicals that they are.

But first, let's look at the basics.

What are hormones?

Much like neurotransmitters, hormones are communication chemicals. However, they are distinct from neurotransmitters in the way they deliver their message.

Hormones travel around the body, not in the central nervous system but in the 'periphery', specifically in the bloodstream or in the fluid around our cells. They are on the lookout for target cells. Once they find their target, they bind to a receptor inside or on the surface of that cell and deliver their instructions, thereby changing the activity of that cell. There's a high degree of specificity involved; hormones can't just land anywhere. If the cell receptor site is the lock, the hormone is the key that fits it.

The stress–hormone connection

In Day 2 you heard about the body's main stress response system: the HPA axis. The hormone system controlling reproduction is the hypothalamic–pituitary–ovarian (HPO) axis. When you're under stress, the HPA axis is prioritized. Cortisol (the main stress hormone) signals to the brain that now is not a good time for reproduction, repair, or even rest.

When the HPA axis is firing constantly, it interferes with the normal ebb and flow of oestrogen and progesterone. Women notice this as late, missed or heavier periods, more PMS, more cramps and increased irritability. Stress also diverts nutrients and hormonal building blocks away from the ovaries and towards survival systems.

Irregular periods, PMS and PCOS

One of the first signs of hormone havoc is changes to the menstrual cycle. Periods may become irregular, lighter, heavier or stop completely (amenorrhoea). PMS symptoms intensify – bloating, breast tenderness, mood swings, headaches, sugar cravings and sleep problems.

Polycystic ovary syndrome (PCOS) is one of the most common hormonal disorders in women of reproductive age. PCOS is strongly linked with insulin resistance and chronic inflammation, both of which are worsened by stress. The result is often irregular or absent periods, acne, unwanted hair growth, difficulty losing weight and fertility problems.

Fertility

Chronic stress signals to the hypothalamus that the environment is not safe for reproduction. Ovulation is delayed or switched off entirely. Without ovulation, progesterone is not produced, which leads to oestrogen dominance and even more PMS symptoms – anger, anxiety, sleep trouble, cravings and low mood.

Thyroid dysfunction

The thyroid is a small gland in the neck, but it controls the speed of your metabolism, heart rate, digestion, temperature and even brain speed. It's finely tuned to stress.

Cortisol suppresses the conversion of inactive thyroid hormone (T4) to active (T3). Chronic stress can lead to symptoms of hypothyroidism (underactivity of the thyroid) including fatigue, weight gain, constipation, brain fog and low mood.

There's also a nutritional component to hypothyroidism: two main building blocks of thyroid hormones are tyrosine – an amino acid derived from protein – and iodine, but many other nutritional components play a part in the creation, conversion and transportation of thyroid hormones too, such as selenium, iron, zinc and vitamin A. Any of these can impact thyroid function if there is a deficiency.

Stress can also trigger or worsen autoimmune thyroid diseases like Hashimoto's or Graves'. Chronic stress increases inflammation and gut permeability, two major contributors to autoimmune conditions. Supporting thyroid health means managing stress, healing the gut and ensuring optimal nutrient status.

Menopause and perimenopause

The transition to menopause (perimenopause) can last up to ten years. Fluctuating levels of oestrogen and progesterone cause hot flushes, night sweats, insomnia, anxiety, memory lapses, low mood and weight changes. Stress amplifies every one of these symptoms.

Oestrogen is anti-inflammatory and supports the production of serotonin, the 'feel-good' neurotransmitter. As oestrogen declines, women become more vulnerable to stress, low mood and anxiety. Progesterone, which is naturally calming and sleep-promoting, drops too, making it harder to switch off at night or recover from setbacks.

During menopause, the adrenal glands take over sex hormone production. But if the adrenals are already depleted from years of chronic stress, this 'backup' system is compromised. Symptoms become more severe and recovery takes longer.

Nutrition, blood sugar and hormone balance

Diet and nutrition are critical to hormone health. Chronic stress often leads to skipped meals, high-sugar or high-caffeine diets, and blood sugar swings. Unstable blood sugar puts more strain on the adrenals, further amplifying hormone chaos.

Protein, healthy fats, leafy greens, nuts, seeds and slow-release carbohydrates are foundational for hormone production and balance. Key nutrients for hormone health include B vitamins, magnesium, zinc, selenium, iodine, vitamin D and omega-3 fats. Without these building blocks, the body can't make enough hormones or keep them in balance.

The gut microbiome also affects hormone metabolism. An unhealthy gut can increase oestrogen recirculation, worsen PMS and add to inflammation. Supporting the gut with fibre, fermented foods and plenty of plants can help restore balance.

Hormone havoc is not inevitable or irreversible. By reducing stress, improving nutrition, supporting gut health and listening to your body, you can restore hormonal balance – even after years of chaos. Sometimes medical treatment is necessary, but lifestyle changes are always part of the solution.

In Day 7, we'll focus on the gut – your 'second brain' – and how it drives hormone, immune and mood health.

So what? Over to you…

1. What patterns have you noticed between your stress levels and your hormones, cycles or symptoms?

2. Which of these connections is most significant for you right now?

3. What's one small act of hormone self-care you could add this week?

Day 7
Gut instinct

Your digestive tract is the interface between you and the outside world.

Most people are aware of the digestive system's role in breaking down and absorbing the food we eat. But did you know that the gut is also the first line of defence in the human immune system and can communicate with our brain to influence our mood and cognitive performance? The digestive tract is also home to a vast microbial ecosystem, known as the gut microbiome: an essential part of our biology that, when balanced, promotes good health and stress resilience.

The gut–brain axis

The gut is frequently referred to as our second brain and is home to at least 100 million interconnected neurons – the largest collection of nerve cells in the human body.

They may seem far apart, but the brain and the gut are connected both physically and chemically – a connection known as the gut–brain axis. Originating in the brain, the vagus nerve connects the gut to the central nervous system and enables bidirectional messaging between the two organs. Similarly, chemical messengers produced in the gut can travel to the brain via the bloodstream and vice versa.

A healthy brain will support digestive health. However, under stress, the burnt-out brain can send unhelpful signals that disrupt digestion and the balance of our gut microbiome. Similarly, a healthy gut, with the help of its bacterial friends, will produce the brain chemicals that regulate mood, memory and attention, whereas a poorly functioning gut or imbalanced microbiome can negatively influence our mental health and be a contributing factor in burnout.

Your digestive system is your immune system's first line of defence. For example, your stomach produces acid that not only aids digestion of food and the breakdown of protein into those essential amino acids but also kills off bacteria that may have arrived from the mouth that shouldn't really be entering the small intestines.

How stress affects digestion

When the body is in 'fight or flight' mode, digestion is down-regulated. Blood is diverted away from the gut to the muscles and brain, stomach acid production drops and enzyme output is reduced. Food isn't broken down or absorbed efficiently, leading to bloating, pain and unpredictable bowel movements.

Over time, this can disrupt the balance of the microbiome – the trillions of bacteria and fungi living in your gut. These microbes help digest food, regulate the immune system and even produce neurotransmitters like serotonin. Chronic stress can lead to a reduction in beneficial bacteria and an overgrowth of less helpful strains.

The burnout sugar rollercoaster

Stress changes our eating habits. Many people crave sugar, caffeine or comfort foods when overwhelmed. Skipped meals, mindless snacking and late-night eating become common. I call this the 'burnout sugar rollercoaster': a quick burst of energy followed by a crash, irritability, hunger and cravings for more.

Mild fluctuations in blood sugar levels are normal and occur within a narrow range that the brain considers safe. When we consume food, it's broken down into smaller components as part of digestion. The digestion of carbohydrates produces glucose (or blood sugar), which is easily absorbed into the bloodstream and acts as the main energy currency for the brain and the rest of the human body. In response to rising glucose levels, the pancreas releases the hormone insulin, which signals to the body that any excess glucose not immediately required for energy should be removed from the blood and stored for later use. Our blood sugar returns to normal levels – happy days.

But rapid spikes in blood sugar from a carbohydrate-dense snack can lead to too much insulin being released, pushing blood sugar levels too low. This triggers the release of cortisol from the adrenal glands. Cortisol's job is to recruit energy in the face of threat – and a drop in blood sugar is just as threatening to survival as a bear! It triggers the conversion of glycogen back into glucose and stimulates our appetite, signalling us to eat to help restore normal blood sugar levels.

This perpetuates the stress response, keeping you in a cycle of highs and lows. Over time, this can lead to increased fatigue, weight gain, insulin resistance and mood swings.

Digestive issues: IBS, bloating and food sensitivities

IBS is one of the most common stress-related conditions. It's diagnosed when other causes have been ruled out but its symptoms – bloating, pain, constipation, diarrhoea, urgency – are all too real.

Gut permeability, sometimes called 'leaky gut', can also increase under stress. This allows partially digested food particles or toxins to enter the bloodstream, which may contribute to inflammation and sensitivities.

My top tips for supporting gut–brain health

1. Manage stress: as we have seen, high stress levels can detrimentally affect digestive function and the composition of our microbiome.

2. Stay hydrated: water is needed to produce a healthy stool and positive mood. Aim for two litres of good-quality water a day.
3. Chew food thoroughly: chewing initiates the digestive process, signalling to the brain that it's time to release digestive enzymes and letting the stomach know to produce stomach acid.
4. Consume bitter foods (rocket, artichoke, radishes, chicory, herbs, etc), which aid digestion and can improve vagal tone.
5. Consume adequate dietary fibre: diets higher in fibre are associated with lower incidence of mood disorders and support healthy digestion in many ways. Fibre can be found in whole, unprocessed foods such as vegetables, fruit and wholegrains.
6. Space meals at four- to five-hour intervals: the digestive system needs time to rest and initiate a digestive tract cleaning process called the 'migrating motor complex' (MMC).
7. Try adding some live probiotic foods to your diet.

8. Reduce triggers of poor gut function where possible:
   a. Sugar
   b. Antacids
   c. Antibiotics
   d. Alcohol
   e. Gluten.

In Day 8, we'll focus on what should be the easiest way to manage burnout but often turns out to be the hardest: sleep and relaxation.

So what? Over to you...

1. What gut symptoms have you noticed during times of stress, and what do they tell you?

2. Which daily food or lifestyle habits help your digestion, and which seem to make things worse?

3. What one change could you make to improve your gut health?

Day 8
Sleep and relaxation

Rest and relaxation are vitally important for mood stability. Ironically, they're also exactly what you feel you don't have time for if you are at Stages 1 or 2 of burnout!

Why sleep matters

Sleep is vitally important time for your body to repair and your brain to decompress, both of which are essential for keeping you resilient. Sleep is the antidote to cortisol and counteracts its metabolic effects in the body.

But the stress–sleep–mood circle can be a vicious one. Feeling anxious can disrupt sleep, which can lead to low mood. In one study, a chronic sleep deficit of six hours in just one week increased levels of the stress hormones adrenaline, noradrenaline and cortisol by 50–80%![19]

You can improve things significantly by practising good sleep hygiene (for example winding down by reading a book or taking a bath, keeping your bedroom clean, cool and dark, avoiding using your mobile phone in bed, not eating less than two hours before bedtime and steering clear of alcohol, a notorious sleep disrupter).

But stress is also a factor. The sleep–wake cycle is governed by the circadian rhythm, an internal clock set by light, movement, temperature and food. Cortisol should be highest in the morning and lowest at night, while melatonin – the sleep hormone – should rise at dusk.

Under chronic stress, this rhythm is lost. High evening cortisol can suppress melatonin, making it hard to fall or stay asleep. (Screens can compound this too: blue light fools the brain into thinking it's daytime, suppressing melatonin.) The result? You're exhausted all day, restless at night.

But it's not just at night that you can get the rest that helps beat burnout: finding time for relaxation in your day is another powerful tool at your disposal.

Active relaxation

By 'active', I don't necessarily mean physically active, but simply consciously engaging in relaxation. And it doesn't need to take long: an average of just ten minutes of active relaxation every day is enough to offset daily life stress![20]

When we consciously relax, we're activating our 'rest-and-digest' (parasympathetic) nervous system, which counteracts our stressed-out sympathetic nervous system. By tapping into the parasympathetic nervous system – even for a short amount of time – you are essentially breaking the circuit of the stress loop, letting the brain know you are safe and prompting it to reinstate healthy bodily function.

So, what does active relaxation actually entail? Well, there many different options but they all involve an element of mindfulness.

What is mindfulness?

Mindfulness is a stress-management technique designed to improve your mood and overall wellbeing. It has been defined as 'the awareness that arises by paying attention on purpose, in the present moment, and non-judgementally'.[21] The origins of mindfulness lie in Buddhism, but the modern practice has been adapted to a set of non-religious tools and techniques. A vast body of research attests to the benefits of mindfulness including focus on addressing occupational exhaustion and improving personal achievement – both dimensions of burnout.[22]

Mindful practices are varied and take time to learn. The key is to find what works for you. Some take longer than others to master. Here are some ideas to try:

- **Yoga.** Particularly helpful restorative practices include 'yin', which involves holding floor-based poses for longer, and 'yoga nidra', almost like a yogic-sleep.
- **Breathwork.** This is a great place to start if you're short of time. Find a quiet spot, close your eyes and breathe in deeply through your nose to a count of six. Feel your lungs expand and allow the breath to get right down to your belly. Exhale in the same steady way to a count of six. Continue for five rounds, by which time you will have been breathing mindfully for one minute. Well done! Next time maybe aim for two minutes and so on, until you are able to complete ten minutes' active relaxation.

- **Meditation.** This does take time to perfect, but there are some great meditation apps out there that enable you to build your meditation practice up gradually at a time that suits you. The main thing is to find a time of day that works for you and set a reminder on your phone to meditate.
- **Tea drinking.** I almost always begin my wellbeing events with a tea ceremony, tapping into the ancient Chinese ritual, where tea was historically drunk as a health tonic and always consumed communally. Whole-leaf tea contains beneficial phytochemicals (bioactive compounds found in plants), and herbal teas such as chamomile and peppermint can support stress relief.

If the idea of tea appeals, hold that thought because in Day 9 we'll turn to food, and how nourishment supports mood, energy and recovery from burnout.

So what? Over to you…

1. How do you feel about rest and sleep – are they priorities or do you see them as optional extras?

2. What changes could you make to your evening routine or daily schedule to support deeper rest?

3. Where might you build in active relaxation for a few minutes each day?

Day 9

Food for mood and energy

I get it: the last thing you may feel like doing right now is changing your diet. Maybe you're living off takeaways because you just can't face your fridge or going to the supermarket. Cooking from scratch? That's for energetic people who've slept.

But you might already be aware that the foods you are eating aren't helpful and are probably perpetuating the misery you feel. If so, great. This is the first step towards change.

Don't worry, we're going to take it slow. I'm not going to ask you to give anything up. We're just going to look at some small adjustments and build up from there, as and when you feel ready.

Hydrate

A nice easy place to begin is to consider your water intake. Did you know your hydration status can influence your mood? Mild dehydration can significantly increase negative feelings such as anger, confusion or depression. Increasing water intake, on the other hand, can reduce feelings of anxiety.

Here's a straightforward and inexpensive change to help tackle the symptoms of burnout: simply fill a large glass in the evening, leave it somewhere visible when you go to bed and drink it as soon as you get up. That first morning water intake before you do anything else serves several purposes: first, and perhaps most importantly, it represents a positive and manageable action that you are taking to tackle overwhelm head on. Second, that single morning glass instantly increases your overall water intake, whatever your starting point is. And finally, it sets you up for a 'good mood day' – firing up both the body and brain.

Once this routine is embedded, find other ways to increase your water intake. Always drink from glass or a stainless-steel bottle not plastic and ideally filter your water to remove any potentially brain-toxic chemicals. Water can be drunk either hot or cold; you can add fruit or vegetable slices to give natural flavour, or try a herbal tea.

The foundations of nutrition

The basic premise of functional medicine is that we're all unique so there's no single 'diet' that can be universally recommended to protect us all from burnout. But by now you've realized the importance of nutrition in biological function – and how poor nutrition can contribute to reduced stress resilience, fatigue, mood dysregulation and burnout.

The good news is that a healthy diet can protect you from these conditions. In one study, a phenomenal 33% of drug-resistant participants achieved complete remission from depression in just 12 weeks when following a healthy diet![23]

In my clinic, we work on five brain-nourishing foundations and then personalize them depending on the individual's needs. Here are my top five dietary basics when it comes to nourishing your body and mind for burnout resilience and overall mental health.

1. **Eat whole foods.** By this I mean foods without a label, predominantly fresh and plant-based, complemented with a small quantity of high-quality fish and meat. Spending slightly more on slightly less should help you to strike the right balance.

2. **Minimize processed foods.** Processed foods containing refined fats and sugars are notorious mood disrupters and perpetuate stress in the body.
3. **Eat the rainbow.** A plate of brightly coloured food is not only pleasing to the eye, it's good for your brain. Consuming diversely coloured foods helps provide access to weird and wonderful stress-busting and fatigue-fighting micronutrients, such as flavonoids and plant phenols, which are beneficial to mental health.
4. **Include low-glycaemic-index foods.** Don't ditch the carbs – you need fibre to help you digest your food effectively and carbs to help protein reach the brain, so it produces those mood-regulating chemicals we talked about in Day 5. Refined flours in pasta and bread can disrupt your blood sugar balance, so swap white rice and pasta for wholegrain or wild varieties, or even a pseudo grain like quinoa.
5. **Follow a Mediterranean eating pattern.** Although there's no universal anti-burnout diet, the Mediterranean eating pattern is a good start: plenty of vegetables and fish, occasional meat, and healthy fats from olive oil, avocado and nuts.

Protein: the foundation for neurotransmitters

As we saw in Day 5, protein provides the building blocks for neurotransmitters like serotonin and dopamine. Without enough protein, the brain struggles to make the chemicals that regulate mood, motivation and sleep. Many women under-eat protein, especially at breakfast.

Good protein sources include eggs, fish, poultry, beans, lentils, nuts, seeds and dairy. Aim for some at every meal – not just dinner.

Micronutrients: the tiny giants

Micronutrients – vitamins and minerals – are required for every chemical reaction in the body, including those that produce energy, balance mood and fight inflammation. The most important for burnout recovery include:

- Vitamin C: essential for adrenal function and easily depleted through stress
- B vitamins (especially B6, B12, folate): crucial for neurotransmitter synthesis and energy
- Magnesium: calms the nervous system, relaxes muscles, supports sleep
- Vitamin D: supports serotonin and dopamine synthesis

- Zinc: needed for hormone production and immune health
- Iron: carries oxygen, prevents fatigue and brain fog.

Leafy greens, colourful vegetables, nuts, seeds, seafood, beans and whole grains are rich sources of these nutrients.

My top mood foods

These foods feature nutrients that help us to manage or prevent the symptoms of burnout.

Avocados

Avocados are rich in the monounsaturated fats that our brains need to function at their best, as well as other mood-boosting nutrients such as folate and magnesium, 'nature's tranquiliser', which are often depleted in burnout.

Oily fish (or chia seeds)

Oily fish is an excellent source of omega-3, an essential fatty acid that the body can't produce and which must be sourced from the diet. There's a wealth of research highlighting the beneficial effect of omega-3 in burnout-related mood disorders.

If you're vegan, you may need an omega-3 supplement but chia seeds are a moderate dietary source of omega-3. In addition, they are a source of fibre, required to feed the 'good bacteria' in our gut.

Broccoli

Broccoli, part of the brassica family, helps us to detoxify excess and used-up hormones in the liver, particularly oestrogen. Broccoli contains folate, which supports the methylation process, and helps channel tryptophan down the right chemical pathway (when stress can send it the wrong way) to make our happy hormone, serotonin.

Quinoa

Quinoa is a source of low-glycaemic-index (GI) carbohydrate, which protects against mood disorders such as depression.[24]

Berries

Berries are a rich source of antioxidants, required by the brain to ward off damage from toxins and other potentially harmful molecules. Polyphenols are a particularly potent type of antioxidant found in berries that help keep the brain plastic and resilient to stress.[25]

Brazil nuts

Brazil nuts contain mental-health-supportive micronutrients such as ellagic acid, a bioactive compound that can exert an antidepressant effect, and selenium, a resilience-enhancing mineral.[26]

Dark chocolate

Dark chocolate (over 70% cacao) can stimulate the release of the feel-good neurotransmitter dopamine and the 'cuddle hormone' oxytocin. Who doesn't feel better after a hug? Dark chocolate is also a source of iron, which helps to deliver oxygen to the brain and regulate the chemical pathways involved in mood and behaviour.

A handful of Brazil nuts and a few squares of dark chocolate make the perfect mood-boosting mid-afternoon snack.

Peppers

Brightly coloured vegetables like peppers are an excellent source of vitamin C, which is required for the synthesis of the mood-regulating neurotransmitters dopamine and serotonin, and which is depleted by chronic stress. Diets containing high amounts of vitamin C have been associated with elevated mood.[27]

Sweet potato

Sweet potato is a rich source of the plant form of vitamin A: beta-carotene. Vitamin A plays a key role in brain and immune function and has been shown to improve depression and fatigue.[28]

Chickpeas

Chickpeas are sometimes called 'nature's Prozac'. They contain the essential amino acid tryptophan – the precursor for the happy hormone, serotonin, and the sleep hormone, melatonin. Hummus spread onto oatcakes makes a great evening snack. The carbohydrates in oatcakes help with tryptophan absorption, ensuring it can reach the brain more easily.[29]

When more help is needed

Some people need extra support – testing for nutrient deficiencies, gut health or hormone imbalances may be helpful in complex cases, and medication may be appropriate sometimes. Professional support – a nutritionist, health coach or doctor – can make a big difference if you're stuck or unsure where to begin. But for most people, simply improving nutrition is the key to beating burnout.

In Day 10, we'll explore thoughts that heal (not harm) – the power of mindset, beliefs and compassion in recovering from burnout.

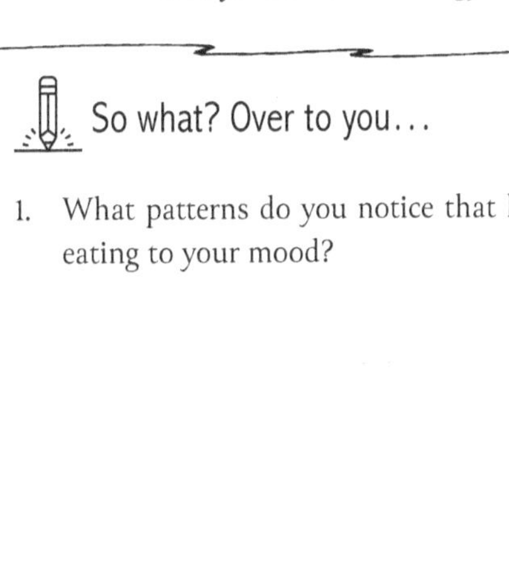

So what? Over to you...

1. What patterns do you notice that link your eating to your mood?

2. In which of these aspects of nutrition might you be most deficient?

3. What's one small, practical change you could make to improve your nutrition this week?

Day 10

Thoughts that heal (not harm)

As we've seen, burnout is most definitely not all in your head. But there's a lot you can do inside your head to beat it! When you learn to identify any limiting beliefs that may be holding you back, and catch and reframe negative thought patterns, you're developing a stress-resilient mindset, helping you to feel more in control.

Reframing is a technique that uses the conscious parts of our brain to reprogramme the subconscious parts. It's about giving the primitive circuitry in your brain new information about the reality of your world to replace the old; reclassifying threat and your ability to cope with it. It's a powerful personal development technique that can improve resilience and support effective performance, and as such, it can form an important part of burnout prevention or regression limitation.

Limiting beliefs

Limiting beliefs are the convictions that we hold about ourselves or the world around us that hinder us from taking opportunities and reaching our full potential. Left unchecked, they can perpetuate a negative state of mind and hyper-vigilance to stress.

Some examples of limiting beliefs might be:

- 'I thrive on stress.'
- 'I'm not a good sleeper.'
- 'I'm too tired to make a change.'
- 'I can't get through the day without chocolate.'
- 'I can't relax without wine.'

They can also run deeper:

- 'I'm not good enough.'
- 'I don't deserve to be happy.'
- 'I'm never going to succeed.'

Limiting beliefs develop throughout our lifetime as a result of our upbringing, education and life experiences. Often these beliefs are not consciously known to us and identifying them might require the support of a therapist, coach or counsellor.

Once you've identified them, you can work on developing alternative beliefs that serve you better. For example:

- 'I am enough.'
- 'I can do anything I set my mind to.'
- 'There are lots of ways I can relax.'

Language

Are you programming yourself to feel bad because of the words you choose?

For example, you might say things like:

- 'I'm terrible for eating chocolate when I am feeling low.'
- 'I'm an idiot for working late.'

When you use language like this, your subconscious mind and belief system are getting the message that you are a terrible person and an idiot. That's not going to help your mood.

Instead, how about:

- 'I'm great at reaching for the biscuits in the afternoon!'
- 'I'm fantastic at getting work done.'

I don't know about you, I feel better already!

Another tip for lifting your mood with language is to enhance the good and diffuse the bad. If someone asks how you're feeling and you reply, 'not bad' when you're actually feeling OK or even good, try saying, 'I feel amazing!' It might sound ridiculous, but using enhanced positive language like this can actually make you feel better – even when your mood doesn't quite match the words.

Diffusing or downgrading negative language can also take the edge off. Instead of 'this project is killing me,' try, 'this project is challenging and is testing me at times.' Can you see how this has downgraded the negative language and thereby diffused its effect on your mood?

Gratitude

One of the best tools for reframing negative thoughts and beliefs is practising gratitude, focusing on what you have instead of what you don't have. So, if your day is weighing heavily on you, take a step back and consider three things you are grateful for.

Gratitude journalling has been shown to lower stress levels and help create a positive mindset.[30] Why not keep a notebook by the side of your bed so you can write down what you feel grateful for before bed and/or first thing in the morning? It's a great way of clearing the brain of negativity.

Connect with something bigger than you

Watch a sunset or sunrise, surround yourself with trees, lie flat and stargaze... There are so many benefits to simply engaging with nature: you are outside in the fresh air; you are contemplating something larger than yourself and you are taking a mindful moment just for you. It can also be beneficial to take time in a sacred place, in private reflection or prayer. Spirituality has been shown to increase resilience to stress, especially as we age.[31]

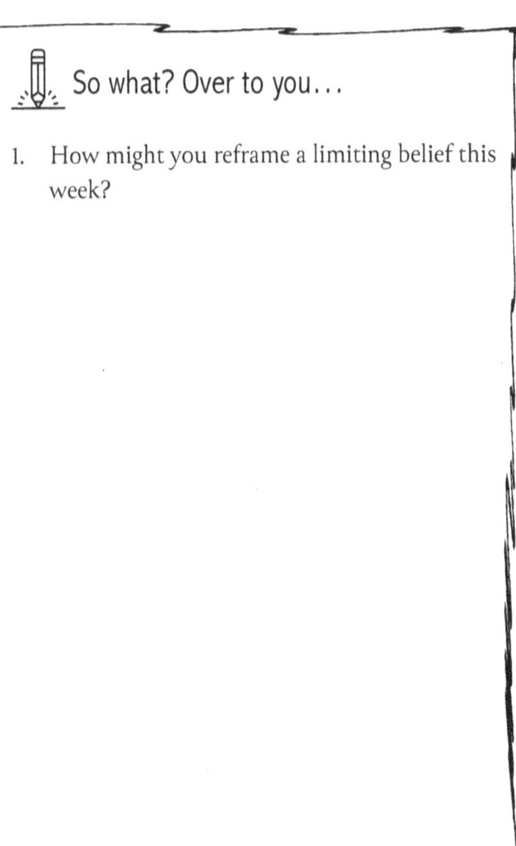

So what? Over to you…

1. How might you reframe a limiting belief this week?

2. What negative language do you use about yourself that you could reframe more positively?

3. Where could you find space for gratitude or reflection this week?

Conclusion

Congratulations on beginning your journey towards beating burnout. Remember, symptoms are warning signals from the brain to get you to change your behaviour. Burnout doesn't have to be inevitable.

There's no quick fix. Managing stress and developing stress resilience through diet and lifestyle change takes time and repetition. It's about establishing and reinforcing new habits and enabling the brain to rewire itself for the better. Nor is burnout necessarily a once-in-a-lifetime experience that, once tackled, will never return.

Burnout recovery and prevention is likely to be an ongoing journey – it certainly is for me. I'm always on the lookout for signs and symptoms that I might be heading back towards burnout again. When I notice something, I take a step back and revisit the principles I have set out in this book. I check in with myself; how am I feeling? What am I thinking? I ask myself:

- Am I getting enough sleep and am I making enough time to actively relax?
- Am I nourishing my body with the right foods to build resilience or has the balance tipped in favour of mood disrupters?
- Are old thought patterns creeping back in that I need to reframe?

I'm not perfect and I don't always get it right. But I'm more aware of my stressors and mood disrupters now. I've learned to recognize the warning signs and symptoms that indicate to me that I might be heading down that road again. I'm also more informed about my personal diet and lifestyle needs when it comes to managing stress and bolstering my resilience levels. I know how to turn my ship around.

Burnout is an entirely unique experience. Your genetics, your life experience and your current health will all determine if and how you experience burnout. Similarly, there's no one-sized approach to preventing it. Take what feels right for you from this book and leave the rest.

Good luck on your journey – and if you want to learn more, head over to our website www.renuclinic.co.uk We'd love to help.

Endnotes

[1] World Health Organization, 'ICD-11 for Mortality and Morbidity Statistics.'

[2] Beauregard et al., 'Gendered pathways to burnout: results from the SALVEO study.'

[3] Taylor et al., 'Biobehavioral responses to stress in females: tend-and-befriend, not fight-or-flight.'

[4] Burnford *Don't Fix Women: The Practical Path to Gender Equality at Work.*

[5] Beauregard et al., 'Gendered pathways to burnout: results from the SALVEO study.'

[6] Lamers et al., 'Evidence for a differential role of HPA-axis function, inflammation and metabolic syndrome in melancholic versus atypical depression.'

[7] Mantella et al., 'Salivary cortisol is associated with diagnosis and severity of late-life generalized anxiety disorder'; Cervantes et al., 'Circadian secretion of cortisol in bipolar disorder.'

[8] Glaser and Kiecolt-Glaser, 'Stress-induced immune dysfunction: implications for health.'

[9] Brzozowski et al., 'Mechanisms by which stress affects the experimental and clinical inflammatory bowel disease (IBD): role of brain-gut axis'; Chang, 'The role of stress on physiologic responses and clinical symptoms in irritable bowel syndrome.'

[10] Kelly et al., 'Breaking down the barriers: the gut microbiome, intestinal permeability and stress-related psychiatric disorders.'

[11] Fasano, 'All disease begins in the (leaky) gut: role of zonulin-mediated gut permeability in the pathogenesis of some chronic inflammatory diseases.'

[12] Tawakol et al., 'Relation between resting amygdalar activity and cardiovascular events: a longitudinal and cohort study.'

[13] Hackett et al., 'Diurnal cortisol patterns, future diabetes, and impaired glucose metabolism in the Whitehall II cohort study'; Kumari et al., 'A nonlinear relationship of generalized and central obesity with diurnal cortisol secretion in the Whitehall II study.'

[14] Nepomnaschy et al., 'Cortisol levels and very early pregnancy loss in humans'; Wainstock et al., 'Prenatal stress and risk of spontaneous abortion'; Sandman et al., 'Corticotrophin-releasing hormone and fetal responses in human pregnancy.'

[15] Lambertini, Chen and Nomura, 'Mitochondrial gene expression profiles are associated with maternal psychosocial stress in pregnancy and infant temperament'; Wu et al., 'Association of elevated maternal psychological distress, altered fetal brain, and offspring cognitive and social-emotional outcomes at 18 months'; Drake, Tang and Nyirenda, 'Mechanisms underlying the role of glucocorticoids in the early life programming of adult disease.'

[16] Hermes et al., 'Social isolation dysregulates endocrine and behavioral stress while increasing malignant burden of spontaneous mammary tumors.'

[17] Sephton et al., 'Diurnal cortisol rhythm as a predictor of breast cancer survival.'

[18] Zarrindast and Khakpai, 'The modulatory role of dopamine in anxiety-like behavior'; Belujon and Grace, 'Dopamine system dysregulation in major depressive disorders.'

[19] Samel, Vejvoda and Maass, 'Sleep deficit and stress hormones in helicopter pilots on 7-day duty for emergency medical services.' PubMed.

[20] Chang et al., 'Effects of abdominal breathing on anxiety, blood pressure, peripheral skin temperature and saturation oxygen of pregnant women in preterm labor'; Ma et al., 'The effect of diaphragmatic breathing on attention, negative affect and stress in healthy adults.'

[21] Kabat-Zinn *Full Catastrophe Living, Revised Edition: How to Cope with Stress, Pain and Illness Using Mindfulness Meditation*, xxxvii.

[22] Janssen et al., 'Effects of mindfulness-based stress reduction on employees' mental health: a systematic review.'

[23] Jacka et al., 'A randomised controlled trial of dietary improvement for adults with major depression (the 'SMILES' Trial).'

[24] Gangwisch et al., 'High glycemic index diet as a risk factor for depression: analyses from the Women's Health Initiative.'

[25] Huang et al., 'Linking what we eat to our mood: a review of diet, dietary antioxidants, and depression.'

[26] Bedel et al., 'The antidepressant-like activity of ellagic acid and its effect on hippocampal brain derived neurotrophic factor levels in mouse depression models.'

[27] Pullar et al., 'High vitamin C status is associated with elevated mood in male tertiary students.'

[28] Bitarafan et al., 'Effect of vitamin A supplementation on fatigue and depression in multiple sclerosis patients: a double-blind placebo-controlled clinical trial.'

[29] Spring, 'Recent research on the behavioral effects of tryptophan and carbohydrate.'

[30] Emmons and McCullough, 'Counting blessings versus burdens: an experimental investigation of gratitude and subjective well-being in daily life.'

[31] Manning et al., 'Spiritual resilience: understanding the protection and promotion of well-being in the later life.'

Enjoyed this?
Then you'll love...

The Burnout Bible by Rachel Philpotts

Winner 2024: The People's Book Prize Beryl Bainbridge Award for First-Time Author

Business Book Awards 2024 Finalist

Are you fed up of feeling tired, wired and unable to manage your mood? Worried that your mental health is having an effect on your relationships or your ability to perform at work?

You are not alone.

Many successful career women believe they thrive under pressure yet become susceptible to the negative effects of stress. Despite unexplained changes in their health, some ignore the warning signs and burn out. At best this leaves them unable to function and at worst it can lead to infertility, heart attack, stroke or dementia.

Enjoyed this? Then you'll love...

Antidepressants are frequently offered for the symptoms of burnout **but there is another way.**

In *The Burnout Bible*, registered nutritionist, functional medicine practitioner and mental health expert Rachel Philpotts shares:

- A simple 4-step solution to improving your mood naturally
- Evidence-based nutrition and lifestyle tips to tackle fatigue and emotional overwhelm
- Quick and easy mood-boosting recipes

All designed to help you beat burnout and feel revitalized, reenergized and restored.

Other *6-Minute Smarts* titles

Building Great Teams (based on *Workshop Culture* by Alison Coward)

Collaborate Better (based on *Collabor(h)ate* by Deb Mashek PhD)

Customer Success Essentials (based on *The Customer Success Pioneer* by Kellie Lucas)

Do Change Better (based on *How to be a Change Superhero* by Lucinda Carney)

Find Your Confidence (based on *Coach Yourself Confident* by Julie Smith)

Find Your Purpose (based on *The Purpose Handbook* by Eloise Skinner)

Get That Promotion (based on *Getting On* by Joanna Gaudoin)

Grow Your Product Business (based on *Tame Your Tiger* by Catherine Erdly)

How to be Happy at Work (based on *My Job Isn't Working!* by Michael Brown)

How to Get to Know Your Customer (based on *Do Penguins Eat Peaches?* by Katie Tucker)

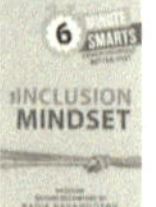

The Inclusion Mindset (based on *Beyond Discomfort* by Nadia Nagamootoo)

The Listening Leader (based on *The Listening Shift* by Janie Van Hool)

Love Your Job (based on *WorkJoy* by Beth Stallwood)

Managing Big Teams (based on *Big Teams* by Tony Llewellyn)

Mastering People Management (based on *Mission: To Manage* by Marianne Page)

No-Fluff Soft Skills (based on *Soft Skills, Hard Results* by Anne Taylor)

No Nonsense PR (based on *Hype Yourself* by Lucy Werner)

Present Like a Pro (based on *Executive Presentations* by Jacqui Harper)

Reimagine Your Career (based on *Work/ Life Flywheel* by Ollie Henderson)

Sales Made Simple (based on *More Sales Please* by Sara Nasser Dalrymple)

The Speed Storytelling Toolkit (based on *Exposure* by Felicity Cowie)

Stay Focused (based on *Attention!* by Rob Hatch)

Write to Think (based on *Exploratory Writing* by Alison Jones)

Look out for more titles coming soon! Visit www.practicalinspiration.com for all our latest titles.

www.ingramcontent.com/pod-product-compliance
Lightning Source LLC
LaVergne TN
LVHW051011080826
845145LV00009B/2566

* 9 7 8 1 7 8 8 6 0 8 9 2 3 *